Poetic Therapy

Collection of Poems by

Michael "Chief" Peterson

Released January 2025

Printed in the United States of America
Cover Design Jamal Wynn
Edited By Sunni Soper
ISBN 978-1-7333152-1-0
Published by 310 Brown Street
www.310brownstreet.com
www.chiefthepoet.com
chiefthepoet@gmail.com

I've recently learned that I operate in "Artist Brain." It wasn't until partnering with people outside of the creative arts realm that I began to accept that "Artist Brain" is REALLY a thing. Of course, it varies amongst us, yet there are similarities we all possess. Regardless of the medium, us artists beat to the sounds of our own drum.

Each piece in this collection is relative to my personal experiences. All are depictions of my thoughts & life transcribed into free verse poetry. No rules, no guidelines, just me, a pencil & my notebook. Oftentimes, one of the main questions I get after or even during performances is "what inspired you to write that poem?" As a result, I've decided to share those ideals & inspirations with you in this book. Prior to every poem you will read an abridgment of why/what inspired each poem to be written.

Writing has been my therapy, & the stage has allowed me to be that voice for the voiceless. Perhaps you may find yourself in the inner workings of my writings & I'm praying it brings a sense of peace to know that you are not alone on this journey.

Poetic Therapy = Messages for those of us who haven't quite grown the confidence to stand strong in our vulnerability.

Contents

Chie

HAIKU
PROGRAMS FOR STUDENTS
BUT THEIR TEACHERS HAVEN'T
HEALED FROM THEIR OWN TRAUMA

Who Am I: A social media challenge during covid got my brain spinning to assess my own identity. I've always prided myself on being a well-rounded man. With that balance comes much contradiction. Defining who we are can be a complex task. I am this poem, that is the story I wished to tell.

Who Am I

Who am I?
My birth name is Michael
It means he who is like God
There's a hint of heaven in every word I write
Therefore, we shall all be blessed tonight. AMEN
But who am I?
With one brother in corrections & the other in a casket
I am my mama's only child
I am the only child my father didn't raise
Pen, pencil & page have been more of a parent than Papa
Let the stone roll where it may
Real life irony, my father's last name is Rolle
Yet who am I?
I am a masterpiece in the making
I am a poet so I can bend words & say things like
I am extrovertedly introverted
I can be the life of the party or just not go to it
I am an alcoholic who's never been drunk a day in his life
I get punch drunk off punchlines
Hit me with your best - verse & not shot
Because Black men don't come back from those
I am an unprepared eulogy at my brother's funeral
I am still living with that regret
I am last month's rent with next week's check
I am Ricky & Bobby - First & last
I am the haves & have nots
I am made it home from the traffic stop
But still hashtag waiting to happen
Can't kneel or stand for my rights
I am hands up & polite & still knee on neck or bullet in back
I am both Miracle & Menace
You say it's a life sentence in this skin, I say it's a win
My melanin be sliced bread & pants with pockets
The best thing since been - since been
My Mama named me Michael Jermaine
You only know me as my a.k.a.
This is the part where I hit you with a gun bar
With one brother gunned & the other barred
I've learned to stay away from them both
I am the truth in a world full of lies
I am Big Mama's eyes & Granddaddy's nose
I am the generational curse & gift

I am a combination of lift every voice & sing & in the words of Crime Mob
As quoted by Urban Negro Philosopher Charlamagne Tha God
I am always ready to knuck if they buck
I am LL Cool J's I need Love & Mama Said Knock You Out
I am Martin's dream & Malcom's by any means
Part lover part wish a nigga would
I am Paradox & oxymoron
You know, kinda like the hate y'all give Lebron, but love you give R. Kelly
I am what comes from the belly of the beast
I am the beast & the beauty within him
I am as good as it gets, but not good enough
Confidence cloaked in insecurity
I am alive to tell my story
Head high, smile full and my mama still proud of me
I'm winning
I am the win within the loss
I am the beginning & the end
Still writing the chapters in the middle
I am the shoe on the wrong foot, but the step in the right direction
I am the broken mirror for little Black boys to see their reflection
I am the dream they see from the windowsill in the projects
I am the project from the projects projected not to make it
I am the one in the family who made it, yet still trying to make it
First to graduate college, but last to have a family
Hella macho & manly, but I cry damn near daily
I am the '*HELL YEAH, LET'S GET IT*' & the '*umm, I don't know, maybe*'
This is who I am & I'm still learning
I'm still learning to love me
I am still -I am learning - I am love -I am me

HAIKU

GREW UP POOR

BLEW OUT CANDLES ON CAKE THEN USED THEM TO LIGHTHOUSE AT NIGHT

Where I'm From: Growing up in the inner city typically comes with a bad reputation. Yet, those same inner-city struggles are what molded me into the man that I am. I've taken the trials of my upbringing & used them as fuel.

Where I'm From

Where I'm from isn't as bad as people always make it seem

Where I'm from kids are finding better ways than breaking the laws, smoking, & drinking

They're now taking a pause, stopping & thinking, making better choices to prepare for their future, cuz living life as a bum is not something they can get used to

Where I'm from some bums dress better than teachers and have more faith than our preachers & since there's no money their life is now featured around violence & crime & half of their time is spent begging for dimes

Yes, the coin & the bag

They'd rather get a drag than a job

Change is what we need so society can breathe a breath of fresh air by knowing our kids care about going to school cuz some rappers have now made it cool to be a drop out

"Mr. Mr., them teachers don't like me" is a cop out

"Them cop's out to get me" is an excuse

Excuse me for telling it like it is, but our kids don't care anymore & I'm blaming it on the parents

Apparently, nothing is being said at home, too many kids feel alone

Where I'm from, if you catch em while they're young, there's still time for change, yet so many have grown stubborn in their ways & now their days are spent behind bars, jail house rap stars, body builders & ballers

I'm just calling it how I see it, cuz I've seen it,

as far as you know I could be it

Where I'm from isn't as bad as people always make it seem

Where I'm from, more kids know how to curse than write cursive & use words like lookeded, hurted & worstest

She told me, "*Mr. Mr., he lookeded gooood, but his girlfriend was the worstest, it hurted my eyes looking at her*"

Where I'm from, most people just laugh & no one wants to correct her

They just choose to neglect her

Which is nothing new cuz so many men have already done it before

Her mother's ex-boyfriend, her father

Her own ex-boyfriend, a father

Her sister's soon to be ex-boyfriend, a father of 3 & 2 on the way & it's so sad to say that too many men in this world have abandoned little girls or little boys for that matter

What ever happened to Daddy's little girl?

Cuz in this world, yes, even where I'm from

I've noticed a pattern with men leaving their young

The saying fits perfect, like father, like son

They weren't taught any better but they learned how to measure, cuz they learned it in the hood

It's all good cuz school is for the birds, so they get high off that herb

& hope Ms. Clark grades with a curve

So they can be the first to pass & graduate

But where I'm from, they're always a tad too late

Where I'm from, if it ain't one thing then it's another

My 13-year-old student got caught smoking weed with her brother

Come to find out she's pregnant & so is her mother

What bothers is, neither one knows who the father is

Around my way, that's just the same story just a different day

I tell my students, listen closely while I school you

Don't let my shirt & tie fool you.

I'm from where you're from, I've done what you've done, seen what you've seen

I was once in between a rock & hard place, just like you

Yeah, my father left me too

I've seen my brother die, watched my mother cry & been too afraid
to try

I've seen my grandmother slapped, my uncle on crack, I've seen a
mother beat up by her daughter

Some honest to God truth, my great-grandfather was
murdered over a quarter

Don't believe me then ask Big Mama

Yeah, I received help from the state

Damn what you say them food stamps were great

Yeah, I've heated my house with the oven & drank Kool-Aid from a
jelly jar & the city bus was once my car

I've faced my share of adversity & overcome it

They can't stop me, I can't lose, cuz I choose not to

If you need help, I got you, we'll make it to the top together then
scream,

Where I'm from isn't as bad as people make it seem

They can take away our dollars,

but they can't take away our dreams

Remember,

where you're from isn't as bad as people always make it seem

HAIKU

TELEVISION SHOWS
ARE BECOMING THE PARENT
IT'S REMOTE CONTROL

Taco: I was watching the NFL draft during the trump campaign. It was right during the turmoil surrounding the building of the wall at the Mexico border. The Dallas Cowboys drafted Taco Charlton out of the University of Michigan & I remember saying to myself. "*The irony in America drafting a Taco, trump probably wants to build a wall around the stadium.*" Thus, a poem was born.

Taco

With the 28th pick in the NFL draft

The Dallas Cowboys selected defensive end Taco Charlton from the

University of Michigan

My first thought

Who the hell would name their kid Taco?

2nd, do you see the irony?

The Dallas Cowboys

America's team, drafts a taco

trump probably wanted to build a wall around the stadium

Taco, 6'6" 277 pounds

Built like Black stallion

America - equestrian a.k.a. Cowboys

Still riding our backs on hopes to be great... again

They call us athletes the jocks

While this country places us on top of America's auction block,

I mean draft

Sending the biggest most athletic Demi-Gods to a team

Where they sacrifice their bodies, in a game,

For a country, that once made a game, of sacrificing their bodies

Makes sense America would draft a taco

We've always been a shell of a country

With the dark meat stuffed at the bottom

Everything else stacked above it

Lettuce (let us) pledge allegiance to the cheddar (money)

At the expense of ground beef (war)

The only way it can ever be deemed supreme is when you add a

layer of white sour cream to the very top

There's a metaphor in that

Fun fact, 81% of NFL quarterbacks are white

Meanwhile, 81% of NFL defensive players are Black

Irony, White men control a ball

Trying to break through a wall of brown faces

There's a history lesson in that

We are the front linebackers

Pushed in the cornerback where we hail Mary for our safety

Praying they don't throw the long bomb

Fun fact: 86% of NFL running backs are Black

91% of the wide receivers are Black

To this day, we're still only believed good enough to run & fetch

I mean catch a pass.

Catch my point?

Irony, Taco went to the University of Michigan - The Wolverines

Taco is an American superhero

With a chip on his shoulder that refuses to die no matter what you throw at him

The taco is one of the main things that makes America great

You can't draft a taco then deport the people that created it

If minorities took back everything we gave this country

America's team would be a lone star

There's no team without us, we make up us

The U.S. ain't complete without us

This country was built on us being less than man

Yet us are the ones who are idolized & made icons

But only if us got us some size or some talent

Even then, us still only get a fraction of what us earn them billionaires

122 major professional sports team

Only ONE Black owned

Irony, white men own the field, Black men work them

There's a history lesson in that

So, when you draft a taco in the first round

You can't treat its people like 2nd class citizens

This country may not like us

But everyone,

EVERYONE,

Loves,

A fuckin Taco

HAIKU

ALL LITTLE CHILDREN
HAVE IMAGINARY FRIENDS
I CALLED MINE DADDY

Do's & Don'ts: During a period of civil unrest, I became overwhelmed with the amount of innocent Black men being murdered for everyone to see. I thought of ways to keep myself & my children from experiencing such a fate. I then created checklist of all the things we've been advised to do. Yet those same things are what have been the causes of   many deaths.

Do's & Don'ts

If you wanna live I suggest you pay attention

I've created a list of do's & don'ts to help sustain your existence

I pray you're listening

I think its best I start with some of the don'ts

Don't chase your dreams they'll say you ran away & shoot you in

your back

Don't stand your ground they'll shoot you in your face

Run! Don't run, speak up for yourself

Don't speak, it will be used against you
If you use your words, they'll say you had a weapon
Don't know the law! They'll say you had weapon

Don't judge, they do it for you

Don't commit crimes, you are one
Don't reach in your pockets

Don't have pockets
Don't put your hands up

Don't have hands
Don't drive to work if your taillight is busted

Don't drive

Don't hunt, for you are the prey

Don't wear black
Don't be Black
Don't be brown
Don't have a tan

Don't pay attention to color
Don't have faith
Don't pray 5 times a day

They'll say it was all your fault
Don't grow a beard
Don't grow up
Don't have braids, locks or an accent
Don't have asthma, I can't breathe either

Don't sell anything.

Not drugs, loosies or cd's,

Do not buy anything

No candy, especially skittles
They say you support rainbows, call you gay & shoot the Orlando out of you

Don't go to night clubs

Don't go out at night

Don't be 12 years old in the park

Don't play with toy guns or real guns
Don't be real
Don't have money, they'll say you stole it
Don't have success, they'll steal it from you
Don't have kids, their lives won't matter

If you do, don't bring em to school or church, they shootin folks

Don't have eyes. For what?
You've seen this 400 years ago
Don't have ears, you've heard this all before
Don't have feelings, they don't
Don't be fast, bullets are faster
Don't have a name, you'll end up being a number
Like 9-24-83 to 2-22-09 10th murder in the 413 that year & it was only February
Don't like February, too many colored folk are attached to it
Don't like guns, too many colored folk are detached from it

Don't have friends, someone might kill them
Don't like my status, too many posts about death
Don't hashtag shit, it won't make a difference
Dead bodies are the only trending topic

Don't watch the video, they're all the same

Colored man slain, Colored woman slayed, Muslims blamed

Can't we all just get along?

Don't believe that shit!

If the gloves don't fit, the shoes always do

Don't worry, be happy

Don't ask me how, just do it

Don't do it, they'll shoot you

Don't shoot, they'll shoot you

Don't fight with your fist

What you should do is

Learn your rights

Be polite

Pray you make it home at night

And If you do, get life insurance

Because tomorrow you might not be so lucky

HAIKU
THE GAME GOES
ROCK PAPER SCISSORS SHOOT
POLICE TOOK THAT LITERALLY

H & M: There was a T-shirt designed by H & M clothier that read "Coolest Monkey in the Jungle." The marketing team thought it would be smart to put the shirt on a beautiful little Black boy & advertise it all over the world. Social media was in an   uproar about it. Thus, another poem was born.

H & M

Another Black boy in a hoodie sets black America on fire

Except this Black boy didn't die

H&M put little Liam Mongo in a hoodie that read 'Coolest Monkey in The Jungle'

Guess nowadays as long as we get paid
Some of us monkeys will still swing from trees only in different ways

His parents crucified on social media

Because everyone has a Pintrest in what's going on,

For the moment

140 characters in a tweet, spaces included

Instead of 100 million characters in the streets faces excluded

Let's hoodie up like the clan

Cuz ain't nothing stronger than a Black man linked to a Black man linked to a Black man propelled by the Black woman, That's progress

In the sixties, a simple protest lasted 2 years

Now it's a social media blast for 2-days

2 weeks, 2 months, 2 years later no one's concerned with the coolest monkey in the jungle anymore

His parents must have gone ape for that check

It must be nice to keep their pockets & stomachs fed

Must have gotten paid in that banana bread

I bet you can't tell me what the H or M stands for

Go ahead I'll wait...

Let's start with His Mama

Gotta wonder what was on Her Mind

Was it more about Having Money or Holding Morals

For H & M, it was simple, when you Hire a Monkey you get

Monkey Business

Aka Gorilla Marketing

That's what happens when you put a Hoodie on Melanin

Just cause US ain't buying em don't mean THEY ain't selling them

We went from being Hung & Mutilated

To Hired & Manipulated

Guess if you wave a few dollars then it's true

Money see, then monkey do

I don't know about you, but I can't stand the way we're viewed

Is it inmates or primates

Both are bold face lies

Black people have always been the face of the Franchise

The frontline of the movement

When that move meant success, somehow, we end up in the

back of the pack 400 years later still got a target & that monkey on

our back

Only now some of us get paid to keep it there

We gotta do better, gotta be better

We sing songs about injustice, but have a hard time harmonizing

for a revolt

It's a hot track for a moment then we evade reality & get back to

our reality shows

Letting little Liam Mongo know that blacks will support him with

no money spending in H&M

Until there's something funny trending on twitter again

To little Liam Mongo,

you went from being paid & made fun of in a photo

To praised & made royalty & this world knows

Little Black boys have always been majestic

To them, it's about knocking you off your throne

Sometimes a hoodie is the closest thing to a crown that little Black

boys own

Just because they can't see the forest through the trees doesn't mean
they can hide your blackness in a hoodie or sleeves
You tell them your blackness is something you will never let go
Your blackness is something you will always set free
Your blackness is something you will forever have & forever bring
The coolest monkey in the jungle has always & forever
will be, KING!!

<u>HAIKU</u>
THERE ARE MORE SYLLABLES
IN THIS HAIKU THAN YEARS
IN A BLACK BOY'S LIFE

REAL TALK: It was the last poem of my feature set at the infamous Nuyorican Poets Café. I asked the crowd what they wanted to hear. The most Brooklynest' cat in the room yelled *"Aye yo, just keep it real son."* In that moment, I knew I had to create something real, but even more so, it had to be that dude's version of New York real. Back to the notebook I went.

REAL TALK

I asked them what they wanted to hear

One dude in the back yelled "just keep it real son"

Okay, I live in a world where I'm supposed to be dead already

Where Freddy Krueger isn't the only person that scares me in my dreams

I'm afraid to go to sleep in fear of having nightmares of my brother's smiling face

His life has been replaced with memories of him laying lifeless on a hospital bed

Or watching the coroner pull his body out of a freezer where frost wrapped his head

So sometimes thinking is the hardest part of my day

Why isn't there a name for a daydream that's bad?

You want me to keep it real?

There's 1 bodega in my hood that sells liquor to kids

2 barbershops that sell drugs

3 middle siblings that are now the only child

4 little girls crying for their father

5-gun shots every night

6 million ways to die

7 seven-year-olds sent to 7-11 at 11 to buy lucky 7 scratch tickets

Try saying that 3 times fast & by the time you're finished another adolescent will be shot over skittles

Now riddle me this

What do you call a parent that sent their 17-year-old child to the store?

Heartbroken

You want me to keep it real?

I got students that eat breakfast, lunch & dinner during 6th period café in school

They're so used to eating sleep for supper

That they nap before going to bed as an appetizer

If they swallowed that food for thought during English class

that would be dessert

The question isn't if that glass is half full or half empty

Its who's going to drink what's left in it, so they have something to

wash down that full course meal of imagination

Some feel incarceration is the only guaranteed way to get 3 meals a

day

Hey, a man's gotta eat

I live in a place where pain grows from the street

This is real talk, there's no metaphors

Have you ever met a four-year-old with Chlamydia?

I have, & we all know how she got it

Mommy's new boyfriend couldn't keep his damn hands to himself

But That's what happens when Daddy's not around

That's what happens when kids are left at home alone

If E.T. can phone home then why the hell couldn't daddy?

Speaking of the phone, I once called a mother to tell her that her

daughter got caught having sex in the school basement

Mom said '*Oh' my God, are you serious? I don't have time to deal*

with this & I'm at work, call her father" then hung up on me

Most people are shocked that she hung up on me.

I was happy her father was in her life

I got two friends with a girlfriend & a wife & kids from em

both

One that had twins outside of his marriage

Got divorced, found out the twins aren't even his,

got back with his wife, they adopted the twins & now they're one

happy family.

I guess that's what you call a catch 22

When you're hiding a lie that ends up becoming the truth

Then, you adopt that lie to become your reality

I guess two wrongs do make a right

Now the question is, is he a good man or a dog?

Or does the candle burn on both ends?

Is judging me or my friend really worth it?

Before you pass judgement make sure you're perfect

Because you asked me to keep it real & suddenly you wanna judge me?

I'm the kid that grew up believing no one ever loved me

The ugly duckling, Cinderella with no prince charming or glass slipper

Just absent parents & two mean sisters

Born to be a quitter like daddy

Just a Black man in the background, a caddy

Never a hole in one except in my sock or in my t-shirt

That was handed down from my sister

I wished for many things

Like a best friend, the exterminator or having heat in the house

What you know about blowing out the candles on your birthday cake

Then using em to light your room at night

Every day in my life has been a fight

Somehow, I live. I live to fight another day

"Shit just got real" is something you'll never hear me say

It didn't just get real, it's always been this way

He asked me to keep it real & I'm just trying to save a soul through a pen

The next time you see me, instead of judging me

Please, tell me, where the hell have you been?

HAIKU
MOM IS MAD CUZ DAUGHTER SMOKED HER WEED
SHE DOESN'T CARE THAT SHE'S PREGNANT

Light Skinned Boy: My first son was born very fair skinned. I knew I was a great father, but struggled internally because his skin didn't look like mine. I kept hearing my southern *aunts "If she can't use your comb, don't bring her home."* My mind began to question my ability to parent a child that doesn't share my melanin. I began to ask myself, what if he's too white for the black family & too black for the white family? What if they call him the N-word? Does he have permission to say the N-word? Do I teach him to take advantage of his privilege?   If it will help him make it home safely, then I absolutely will. I then poured my confusion into my notebook.

Light Skinned Boy

Light skinned vs dark skinned is all fun & games
Until my son was born white
My dilemma in life is will I only raise him to be half right?
Will he have little white boy problems that grow into big Black
man insecurities?
Will I have to prepare him for when security follows him through
the mall?
Or will his 'privilege' let him shop in peace?
Will I be less worried about him being shot in the streets & trust
his 'privilege' will bring him home?
He has light skin, big, beautiful, brown eyes, kinky curly hair,
my nose & he just turned 10
I'm confused on what lessons to teach
I fear his white skin will make him the black sheep
The streets will say he's not black enough for the hood but not
white enough to wear one
My friends say I've created this issue & society doesn't care
But everywhere we go I can feel the stares burning through the
flesh of my flesh
He is the blood of my blood, but I must confess,
Maybe I did create this issue over his color
I didn't know what to expect
Sometimes a pen is just as good as a mirror when it's time to
reflect
I try to see his problems before he even has any
I don't know what little white boys go through as kids
So, I interview my students,
Bobby says they'll let him slide & he'll be safe
As long as no one knows home base is black

I'm trying to gain insight on what it's like when they play outside
Is their plight still the same?
Can they still play their game when the streetlights come on?
My son will make it home, but his shadow will get arrested
Society expected me not to be there in the first place
I'm supposed to be doing life, not raising one
They see felon instead of father
They see skin instead of kin
They're more used to a Black man carrying sin instead of his son
Our skin may not match, but our DNA does
So do not act shocked when you see us together
I never imagined being a parent would be this hard
It's difficult to play the hand you're dealt while society shuffles
race cards
But the Black Jack is always a winning hand
I'm just worried about how many times my son will be hit trying to
reach 21
Yet this is no game. I am his father not his coach
They say white boys are only delivered into the hands of Black
men when there's a chance of athletic promise
I promise to teach him to be a man, to be honest, to be genuine,
to never lie & that color should never matter
Unfortunately, it's a matter of fact, being any kind of black today
is a crime
You either end up serving time or your time is ended
Served with the silver bullet instead of spoon
My friends say I've created this issue & maybe I did
I'm just trying to raise my kid to be the best man he can
How do I raise my son to be something I'm still trying to understand?
Even still, I will look him in his eyes, preach like it's scripture
I named you Major, you are not other

Don't let them check you in that box because they can't think
outside of it
Do not let them feel your hair
When they stare, you stare back, then smile
If you ever get called the N-word, remind them of their ignorance,
then smile
They don't need to know which parent is the black one
Your sister is not your half-sister, she is your blood
You are not half anything, not mutt mulatto or mixed breed
Not coon, cracker, or colored
You are whole, the whole hue & man, you are human
When they ask you what you are,
Ask them who they are, then smile
Tell them you are the best of both worlds
My friends say, I've created this issue based off what society may
see
Truth is, I hope my son stays white
Because the less he looks like his father, the safer he'll be

HAIKU
NO WORRIES OF BOYS
I FEAR MY DAUGHTER WILL WANT
SKITTLES & ICED TEA

Hashtag: Scrolling Instagram & every other post is another Black person killed by the hands of police. It was hurtful. I remember seeing pictures & videos of protests in other cities & all the Black Lives Matter signs displayed hashtags with every one of their names. I thought to myself, "the hashtag says Black lives matter, but the toe-tag attached to their foot shows otherwise." I loved the line & a poem was created.

Fun fact: I was fortunate enough to perform this poem on national television with my now very good friend & Grammy nominated poet Prentice Powell & Def Poetry Jam superstar & poetry icon, The Legendary Black Ice.

Hashtag

The hashtag says Black lives matter
The toe tag says they don't
We've been labeled & tagged
They put bullet holes through the price tag on our lives because to
them we have no value
So welcome to Black Friday
Where the best things in life are free, except air
Nowadays the men are waiting to exhale too
The cops shop, I mean strangle, I mean shoot til we drop
Then call for back up instead of an ambulance
There's an Amber Alert for common sense

A bullseye is pressed on the backs of all Black men
You'd rather press the red dot on your phone to record the Red Dot
aimed at his head instead of calling the Red Cross
As his blood lines the streets & his bloodline is ceased
You use your blood line to tag his peeps in the video you just uploaded
to Facebook
Which won't matter because cops don't FaceTime so let's face facts
When it comes to blacks too many are being tagged by the trigger

Maybe more cops should be on twitter since they love to follow
& retweet, I mean re-beat, I mean repeat the plight of the Black man
Hashtag brown Mike & not the one from Ferguson, but Betty's son

My former student who was killed over drugs

Hashtag Rekia Boyd, Hashtag Philando, Hashtag Oscar

Then there's Julian Cartie
Notice he didn't get a hashtag?
And he was a US Army vet.

All he gets is an unsolved murder and my memory of identifying my
brothers body as they unzipped that black bag and a casket draped in
an American flag that they handed my mother, before they lowered my
brother, into the ground
Pound, Trayvon Martin – Pound, Prince Jones
I admit his name I had to google on my phone
Because I've never claimed to be an activist or a revolutionary
It's just scary how social media dictates the world's trending topics
but we drop it a week later because some football player hit his wife

in an elevator & now we have something new to post about
Foreign or domestic, violence is nothing to joke about
When the weight of the world is measured by the pound sign you

begin to wonder how many hashtags it takes to fill a coffin
Black lives only matter during Black History Month
But Blacks become history so often, we should dedicate a season
Spring's showers lead to Summer's flowers for the fallen
Winter just reminds everyone how cold this world is
Hashtag, our girls is still missing
We were on a mission to find Saddam in a hole in the ground,
Osama at zero dark 30
276 girls get taken from school & they're only worthy of a pound sign
instead of a search party
Pardon my French, but we-we didn't do a damn thing to help those
people in France either

They didn't even get a hashtag
Over 2000 burned alive in Nigeria they didn't even get body bags
Instead, like a flag at half-mast, we let the black ash just blow in the
wind
We can front & pretend with these marches, but we're only pounding
pavement
"I CANT BREATHE" should have been the statement that saved his
life, instead it was the end of his road
Man down, it's funny how Black lives only matter when they come
after the pound
I feel like the only way you know we exist is because our lifelines get
posted in your timelines & because it allows you to share,   you can
act like you care
Do Black lives really matter or will we continue to be viewed as this
country's cancer?
Take a minute, think about it,
Then you can hashtag your answer

HAIKU
BEING A FATHER
BY FAR MY GREATEST BLESSING
P.S. FUCK THEM KIDS

The Talk: A social media prompt during quarantine due to covid. It was geared to be a conversation Black fathers have with their children around the senseless acts of police violence in the world. It's intended to speak to them in a way they would understand. Afterall, isn't it a right of passage for a father to speak to his youngins about the Birds & Bees?

The Talk

Son it's time we talked about the birds & the bees

First, I need you to believe that you too can fly

Most importantly how to protect your wings from some bees cuz
they sting

There are many dangerous animals outside of our nest

That think they can just invade our tree because their branch is
bigger than ours

What do you do when animals attack?

No sudden movements

They may not understand you when you speak but they know what
fear looks like & that invites them closer

Close your mouth & open your eyes

See if you can tell what hives these bees come from

Not all of them sting but I'm guessing they've seen your wings

They know you can fly & sing beautiful melodies

They can only fly & buzz, so they'll try to bust your shell before
you've fully hatched

This concrete jungle is full of traps

There are many snakes in the streets that hide in plain sight

They invite you to trust & believe in them, they're bluffing they're
chameleons

They never show their true colors, but attack you because of yours

I must teach you to defend yourself

Your tone of voice can resolve problems caused by your tone of skin

It's your words that will spare you

Some animals lack the integrity to interact with the intelligent

They use intimidation to scare you. You will stand firm

You will be smart enough to know that sometimes the early bird
loses his worm to the bully, but you will take no bull & learn to

claw your way out the pits

It's a dog-eat-dog world where uniformed K9s are ready to sink their teeth into your dreams

They only attack if you threaten their pride, I mean hives

No, you don't have 9 lives, you're just the black cat with bad luck

What sucks is if you ever get bit, they can just weasel their way out of it

But Back to these bees.

They earn their stripes by putting you in them

Some see Black & White instead of wrong & right

If you type *why do bees attack* into the worldwide spider web

It says, & I quote "experience has shown Bees tend to attack dark things" Now that stings - But it is what it is

Where we're from we learn to dance with wolves & we hide from pigs

What do you do when animals attack?

You stand your ground - Spread your wings slowly

Speak softly - Tell them you are still learning to fly

That you only fight with your words not your fists

but you've seen this happen to too many of your flock and with you it may not stop, but one day it will end

If you should die today, then God will mend your wings in heaven

I told you in the beginning you must believe that you too can fly

Remind these buzzards, that once they sting you,

The bee instantly begins to die too

HAIKU
HE MURDERED MY BROTHER
NOW MY KIDS THINK
THEIR UNCLE IS A TOMBSTONE

So They Can See You: I wasn't going to enter this piece into the book, but why not insert a "love poem" in between these perhaps, heavy pieces? It was inspired by poet extraordinaire "Olusanya" I was watching him perform at an event in Connecticut. In his poem he said "As she lay, I blew gentle breezes over her body. Then, like a blind man reading braille, I ran my fingertips over her goosebumps so I could read her body language & come to understand the story of her flesh" It made me appreciate the skill, imagery & craftsmanship of his writing. I wanted to give people that same feeling & this is my attempt at it.

So They Can See You

When you're in an airplane & you look down & see that real, tiny, miniscule dot
on the ground, that's her
When you squint your eyes to read that fine print at the bottom of the
page, that's her
When you wake up in the morning & can't quite remember what it was you
dreamed about the night before, you were dreaming of her
When you think of beauty, you think of her
When you define beauty, you're defining her
By definition, she is beauty, owns beauty, was beauty, does beauty & this is what
she does to me
I'll tell my lady, whoever said you were fine, must not have known much about
beauty
If they called you cutie, they lied, said you were pretty, wasn't honest,
Cuz you're definitely all of the above, all that & then some,
infinite beauty, plus 1 or 2 or 3 hundred more infinities, because beauty is what
you are.
You own beauty, you've known beauty, you do beauty & this is what you do to me.
I'll tell my lady, I'm so happy & proud to be your man that when I'm not with
you, I wear a T-shirt with your picture on it just to show off your face , so they
can see you
I wanna place you on a trophy, or on a pedestal, or at the tip of a skyscraper, or
on the peak of a mountain,
BETTER YET...
I wanna ask God if he can place you in his hand & hold you in front of the sun
so the world can see you shine
20/20 vision isn't enough, when you're in my arms, I wanna use binoculars just
to make you, that, much, closer
 If I were blind at birth, I still be able to see your beauty,
BETTER YET...

41

I'd rather have sight for just one moment so I could see your face,

Then be instantly blinded so your face is the only image I can ever see again

Your beauty confuses people, it distorts the norm, goes against the grain

It can make a mime start to speak, make angels look scary, turn Batman to a canary, make a bald man feel hairy & when Harry met Sally he was mad, because she wasn't you.

I'll tell my lady, I imagine your beauty as pure white snowflakes during the climax of a blizzard & wish to be trapped in an igloo, naked, so you completely surround me, or as the thickest raindrops during a thunderstorm so when I look out my window, I can't see past you..

Your beauty eases my pain, settles my nerves, so I think everyone deserves a pair of my eyes so they can see you

BETTER YET...

When we make eye contact, I wanna tear out both of our eyes & replace mine with yours so I can look back into my own & see your reflection

I'll tell my friends, I don't need a camera.

I'll mentally develop her photo & process the picture within my chest

When I take off my shirt, her picture will beam like the superman "S"

YES, I want you to see her

So you can see her I've sent her to the moon & bought everyone telescopes so you can see something that's literally out of this world.

You've heard it before, shoot for the moon, if you miss you'll still be a star

She's somewhere near Mars

BETTER YET...

she's my Venus & got me wrapped like

Saturn so together we have a pattern like ... planetary alignment.

It's gotten so bad, I even placed her in the bezel of my watch so like the hands of time, there's no escaping her.

It's gotten so bad, I got kicked out of night school for day dreaming about her

By definition, she is beauty, owns beauty, was beauty, does beauty & this is what she does to me.

It hurts me when I'm with her because.... I have to blink

And for that split second, I can't see her,

So I've tattooed her picture in the inside of my eyelids, so she's always in sight.

As I walk these busy streets bumping into people,

Don't get mad,

Just understand,

I walk with my eyes closed,

Admiring beauty

HAIKU

BEEN DEEPLY LOVED & CHERISHED
MY WHOLE LIFE
BY ALL OF THE WRONG PEOPLE

Product of Pain: An online prompt during quarantine. I don't exactly remember who initiated the prompt but shout out to them because hella poets wrote to this prompt. I'm familiar with various levels of pain so I put it on paper because the prompt said it was ok.

Product of Pain

I am a product of pain
I'm not ready to die so I push past the pain
I am the abortion gone wrong
I was pushed through pain
At 31, my father looked me in my eyes & told me the reason why he
wasn't around is because he told my mother not to have me
Tell me that ain't pain
Wasn't like he had to push
But I pushed through, praying I was bulletproof
Because my brother wasn't
No Luke Cage in him
But will always be superhero to me
At 25, he couldn't survive the pain of a bullet
Casket heavy with sorrow
Future as hopeful as a eulogy
My journal, each page, a tombstone
Full...... of life sentences
Way too many question marks not enough happy endings

I am a product of pain
Pain is what you read about
What we write for
The reason we get drunk & high on
What we live & die with
Never seek but always hide from
Like pain don't have a key to the crib
Like fear don't make deliveries
Like adversity ain't our neighbor
Like struggle don't rent across the street
Like depression ain't the landlord
Like racism don't own the block
When you're stuck between rock & rock all you know is hard place

I am a product of pain
Grew up in a cold world
And the furnace didn't work
Ain't no metaphor in that
We don't talk about this icebox where our hearts used to be
We ain't talkin bout how Black men have become our own enemies
How we still have to find the energy to fight the rest of the world
when our mirror is enough
All's my life I had to push

Pain been pushin back like a bully
He picks on my mama too

I am a product of pain
But my Mama say P.U.S.H.
Pray Until Something Happens
Sometimes you just gotta let the lord deal with it
But you can't bring fists to a faith fight

I am a product of pain
But I got babies that need to know healing is possible
That change gon' come when you look pain in the face
That our reality may be worse than their nightmares
But when you push past pain
It teaches struggle ain't so bad after all
Pain is what gives us purpose
When you realize what your worth is
You understand that pain is a lot different than what hurt is
You keep fighting
You keep dreaming
You keep pushin
Don't you ever stop pushin
Even when it hurts, don't you ever stop pushin
I am A Product Of pain
And I ain't gon' never stop pushin

HAIKU
DAD LEFT
I TAUGHT MYSELF TO RIDE A BIKE
I WISH LIFE HAD TRAINING WHEELS

How To Love Black Man in 10.5 Steps: I have about 5 different versions of this poem. I wanted so bad for it to be a spoken word piece, but it didn't land well in front of a crowd. I'm still working with it for the stage, but I do believe it may be better on the page. I did love the metaphors & similes used, so I figured someone else may love them as well.

Love us & l-ve us hard. We need it.

How To Love Black Man in 10.5 Steps

ONE- Pray for him
The level of love necessary to keep him grounded has to be heaven sent
Be a Godsend, pray for him without preying on him
He may not always see the God in him
As quick as he sees the predator in you
Your prayers are a part of the process, that propel him to push past the pain & pursue purpose with passion
Prayer is action, remind him to not just act
He won't always see the God in him
He will need you speak to God for him

TWO- Take time to understand him
Comprehend the weight of his skin
The heaviness hovering his hue haunts him everywhere he goes
it is hard to harvest harmony between the heaven in his heart & hell in his head
He hopes to be held in high regard
Because humanity often holds him back

THREE- R-E-S-P-E-C-T
Find out what it means to him
He may define it as defying manhood
But can't really explain what manhood is
He will have a hard time separating the truth from disrespect
It's complex, as intimate as love, it's ego easily bruised
Fragile heart built of popsicles curated in the icebox in his chest
It's learning the balance between what he expects vs what he'll accept

FOUR- Speak life into him
He often constructs everyone else's dreams, seldom his own
We are terrible at taking our own advice
Words of affirmation are power tools used to build his backbone
Remind him to not let this country chainsaw his character
Your words, the crane that frame the structure of his nature
Your mouth, the cement confidence in his foundation
Your voice be drilled into his head reminding him
He is tough as nails & not to be screwed with

FIVE- Feed him
Yes, this is literally about food
It's a universal language
I love you can be a hot plate from a warm heart

SIX- Fight for him not against him
The world threw jabs at Michael B Jordan over getting hugged by
Jonathan Majors
They'd rather see us duke it out like Donny & Dame
As if it isn't our Creed to love thy neighbor
They want us sluggers instead of huggers
We tired of being fighters instead of lovers
Love us when our back's against the rope
Be ringside when the heavyweight of the world spars with our
mental
When our minds have gone southpaw don't count us out
Weigh-in when we are ready to throw in the towel
We need you in our corner
Or our bout with love will forever be Rocky

SEVEN- If you are going to fight against him, fight fair
This is about cheap shots & hitting below the belt
It's about how you shoulder roll his feelings
It feels like an argument turned fistfight
Low blows aren't the only form of a body shot
Sometimes your words gut punch, he'd rather be chin checked
Then reflect on the disrespect you spit out your mouth
It's not you vs he, it's the two of you vs the problem

EIGHT- Show him you trust him
When you ask a question, & he's answered your question
Don't question his answer
He's already spent enough time trying to prove himself to his
mirror & the rest of the world
Trust his decision making, his intuition & ability to lead
If he ever tells you, he can't breathe, believe him
On bended knee has a different meaning for us
You think propose, we think we're doing just fine then the water
runs dry. One sweet day turns to the end of the road
Truth be told turning Boyz II Men is only a prayer,
A song for mama, ballad for boys who couldn't be all they could
be because people can't trust past what they can see
He's feared for his fierce exterior
His interior is in fear of feeling inferior
Not having to keep an eye over his shoulder
Allows him to keep an eye on the prize

Showing him you trust him allows him to feel safe

NINE- Be a safe space
Lowering his guard doesn't come easy
When he opens the gates to show you where the kid in the king live
Don't force him to raise drawbridge
He leaves daily to topple giants & conquer castles
He should not return to find a war at the threshold of his front door

TEN- Forgive Him
Don't use a magnifying glass to dissect him
He will not be perfect, mistakes are bound to happen
The chips are only against him if you stack them
To try-try again is how he becomes a man
Relationships don't end when people run out of love
It ends when people run out of mercy
He will need your grace in order to be great

10.5- Don't be Naive
I wasn't only speaking to women. Men, this message is for you too

HAIKU
AFRAID OF JUDGMENT
CRY DRINK DRUGS REPEAT
ALL BLACK MEN NEED THERAPY

Heavy: Inspired by former CT Grand Slam Champion "Decipher." She was working on a piece about her relationship with the gym & church & we tried to make it into a group piece for the slam team. It didn't work out & she had it on the shelf. I was going through some inner struggles & asked her if I could dust off the poem & work in it. It's very relative to who I am & one of my favorite pieces now.

HEAVY

I've been told everything I write has that kinda 'heavy' sense to it
When you carry the weight of the world on your shoulders
The blessings & burden of family on your back
Guilt in your heart
A combination of children, work, finances & fear of being shot, all
while being black
Your pen becomes exactly that,
Heavy
As a Black man in America it's difficult to keep a smile on our faces
We do it anyway
Sometimes carrying this skin is too heavy to bare
We do it anyway
They've only cared about our muscle, but our struggle has become
our strength
But who do we lean on when things get tough for us?
Black men ain't taught to talk about it
Friends say I should write
Fellas say hit the weights
Family says pray
I've become the holy trinity of therapy for Black men
Poet, pastor & personal trainer
Yet what I've learned about slam, the gym & church
Are the pressures to be perfect & develop a praiseworthy body of
work
I must get as close to 10 as possible
That's the score, sets & commandments
But get crucified if the disciples don't believe in my work or word

I work with the weight of the words I put in these bars before they
snap
Because sometimes, they heavy
As in the hand that holds the pen
The man that carries the sin
The vein that joy & pain are in
Black men ain't taught to talk about it
My people say write, pray or lift weights
Yet both the church & the gym come with books of Judges depending on how much is on the plate
People still in their Genesis, think they can Chronicle my Revelations, but don't know what I keep in Psalm helps me do Numbers & make an Exodus from these stressful Acts of life
I'm preachin yall
I've worked hard to build this faith & this muscle & still have trouble pressing off the pressure
Oftentimes I curl up in my pew & shrug it off
Dip depression & push-up prayers hoping God heard me
What goes up must come down - a Burpee
Leaving me standing there
Hand shakin', heart racin' & sweatin'
Second guessing if writing, prayer or working out is working out
I lift prayer, push weights & pen poems
Hoping my bars are as hard as my arms, so I can protect myself from the lies, scores & stones you throw
Black men ain't taught to talk about it
Judged when we do, judged when we write, judged when we lift,
judged when we pray, judged if we cry
I wipe my tears with the same cloth I'm cut from
That's why my skin so rough
When enough becomes enough is usually breakfast for us
Served a plate of pain
Life often scrambled & over-easy
Cup runeth over with stress
Too heavy for the table so we hold that up, too

The bible says the meek shall inherit the earth
What about the bevy of burdens that come with it?
Black men ain't taught to talk about it
My pen turns spotter to help release this gift
If this poem don't make you feel resurrected, call it a dead-lift
You welcome me to the church, the gym & the slam
Say come as I am, it's a judgment free zone
It ain't about the points it's about the poem
But I can't even write one without being judged,
oftentimes by myself
I ain't never been taught to talk about it just told to hide the
heavy
We wear it so you don't have to
We carry it so you don't have to
In the name of the poet, the pastor & personal trainer,
We pray, a man is strong enough to carry the weight of the
world
on his shoulders
Cuz ain't a scale that can measure that
The expectation is to gain faith, lose weight & replace this pain
with poetry
The pen has been my support beam
It keeps me upright -row
Chin up -so, the world can't see me frown
If a Black man falls in the forest does his trauma make a sound?
Since the beginning of time the Black man has always had to
pick
things up never realizing how much it weighs us down
We physically lose weight, but every day we put on pounds
But I've learned to acknowledge, accept & respect the fact
That heavy, will always be the head that wears the crown

HAIKU

RATHER PRAY, & FIND OUT
THERE'S NO GOD
THAN NOT PRAY
& FIND OUT THERE IS

These next few pieces are my testimonies through trial. Life was kicking my ass for a few years, but I made it through.

Ashes To Ashes: One of the most difficult pieces I've ever written. Raw & unchanneled emotion poured from the deepest parts of my being. February 22nd, 2009. One of the worst days of my life. This piece is a depiction of my reality in dealing with one of the greatest adversities life can bring us. It is an excerpt from my One-man play titled "I Wish Life Had Training Wheels" I had to find a way to get this piece out of me. It took me 2.5 years to finally be

able to write it.

Ashes To Ashes

Do you know what it's like to live life with only half your soul
Whereas each year passes
You only grow a half year old
Where everyone expects you to make a half a whole
Over 5,662 (8/24/24) days(from the days I wrote this poem) my little brother was murdered
Young innocent man
Shot right through his hand straight to his heart
February 22nd, 2009, 2:47am the banging begins
"Mike, Mike, it's me Selwyn, Open, They Kill Julian, them kill my son"
What?
"Them kill Julian, shot him 4-time"
I've never felt pain like this before
I've never been drained like this before
Do you know what it's like when your heart feels sore
This is a literal pain that is so hard to explain
It just hurts
Think of the worst pain you ever felt
To the 10th power, squared
It's just not fair
For anyone especially me
28, expected to be the man of the family & keep everybody together
I'd never been to a funeral before
Never had to identify a body, make the arrangements, pick a casket & bury my brother
I did it for my mother cuz that's something no parent should have to go through
But when you serve as everyone else's rock
Who's there to support you?
It was imbedded in my heart that a man's family is his strength and I'm not as strong as I thought I was
I can see why people turn to drugs
I'd take any pill, medicine, shot, I mean needle,
To make this pain go away
Do you know what it's like to question your faith?
To sincerely believe in your heart that God made a mistake
I need help,
Not for myself
No parent wants to outlive their child
I've never really seen my mom cry
I tried to be strong for her
She was trying to be strong for me

But we couldn't hide it
Reality sucks, especially cuz you can't fight it
It creeps up on you at the worst moments,
Especially at night
Playing cards with the fam.... Tears
Playing ball with the fellas.... Tears
At work .... Tears
Kicking back with my lady.... Tears
Talking to my mom... Pain, then the tears
You ever been so sincere in your heart to help someone yet you're not
sure how they will react?
Two specific moments replay in my mind & I wish I could take one
back
I said, *"Mom, what do you want for your birthday?"*
She said, *"I want my son back"*
That shit tore me apart
It's a literal pain that is so hard to explain.... It just, hurts
Think of the worst pain you ever felt
It's worse
But what else did I expect her to say?
My youngest brother Damon, has a shrine of Julian in his bedroom
That my mom avoids looking at
She always looks around
The walls in her house are bare
She took all his pictures down
She told me as she was cleaning one day
She thought she heard a sound
She looked towards the shrine
Julian's voice chimed through
He said, *"Mom, look at me, I'm your son, too"*
She instantly broke down
Sometimes silence isn't the worst sound
We hear voices all the time now
We were supposed to go play cards that night
But some joker wanted to be jackass after the club
Shot my Ace in his heart
Now a part of me is missing
Like a paper with no pen
A child with no father
An angel with one wing
It seems like this pain will never go away
It's a literal pain that's so hard to explain
Grant me the serenity to accept the things I cannot change
I believe heaven is a better place,
But it hurts like hell
I'd give anything for a hug

I'd do anything for a touch
He's with me everyday
But I miss him so much
Please don't feel sorry for me & my family
Just say a prayer for us
Now, the holy trinity has been given another
In the name of The Father, The Son,
The Holy Spirit & My Brother
He's in a better place now & in God we're supposed to trust
Ashes to ashes
And Dust to dust

HAIKU

LEGS THICK LIKE TREE TRUNKS
BIG OL' ROUND BUBBLE BOOTY
HIPPOPOTUMUS

Conversation with God: Another excerpt from my One-man play titled "I wish Life Had Training Wheels" It was designed for the stage, but I wanted to share it because I had this conversation with God & it helped me dig myself out of a depression. He spoke to me in poetry.

Conversation With God

Chief:
God, I need you more than ever I'm at the end of my rope
I'm worried about my mom & I know you can help us both
I've been dealing with a pain that just won't go away
I wear a smile that's phony so I'm faking every day
I need a hand or a hug or just some comfort from a friend
It seems like I'm the only one there for me in the end
I've been stressed beyond belief & cry like I'm two
I've gone so long by myself, its time I turn to you ... again

God:
My son I know your pain & what you've been going through
I've prepared you for hardship, struggle & adversity too
We've dealt with hurt before & overcome challenge together
I've heard your tears, held your pain & helped you get better
The pain will soon cease, yet may never go away
I've built you to be strong & you'll get stronger as you pray
I know you may feel alone & place all burdens on yourself
I've built you to be strong as an image of myself

Chief:
Thank you God I understand all that you have done
Did you have to take my brother? Couldn't I have been the one?
I cursed you for a moment, I questioned my faith
I told everyone in church that God has made a mistake
You gave me someone special that comforted me at the time
I question if it was just for then or will she forever be mine
I ask a million questions, seek guidance & advice
Lord I need you by my side to guide me through this life

God:
I will not apologize for anything I have done
I would never give you anything you couldn't overcome
Don't question my acts nor challenge my wisdom
I built you to be strong & be the best you can be
You know in your heart you can't succeed without me

Chief:
I understand & I'm sorry, but it hurts, I swear it does
You built me to be strong, but I'm not as strong as I thought I was

61

I know I'm not the only one with problems
I know everyone turns to you to solve them
I imagine your burden & the stress on your shoulders
I've heard the glory of life is in the eye of the beholder

God:
I'm glad you understand & I appreciate your faith
I am God of all Gods & I make no mistakes
Count your blessings stay strong & keep me in your heart
Your brother is with me now & has a brand new start
Your father I will deal with, his eyes will open wide
Your mom I will comfort & her pain will subside
Your relationship I will heal, love will remain in your favor
Don't run from the emotion I ask you to love thy neighbor
Stand firm in your faith don't ever question my word
I will deliver on my promises & to doubt me is absurd

Chief:
I will pray & be strong & keep you first in my life.
If the day ever goes wrong, I will never think twice
Can you please help my heart cuz pain hurts my soul.
I know there is a plan for me & soon it will unfold
You built me to be strong & that's exactly what I will be.
Thank you for this talk & for believing in me.
I believe in myself & know there's nothing I can't do
I will never be alone because I will always have you

HAIKU

VIDEO GAMES
WERE THE CAUSE OF OUR BREAKUP
NOW I MISS MY EX-BOX

Hard Things: In dealing with such grief, there's an added layer that comes when having to explain the circumstances to your children. My daughter wasn't born when it happened. As she grew, I began to tell her stories of her uncle & took her to see him often. The innocence of a child had her genuinely believing that her uncle was in fact, the tombstone we would visit. It was endearing yet heartbreaking to learn of. Thus, this poem was written.

Hard Things

There's a 7-year-old crying over a man she's never met
As if they held hands in an after-life before her life even began
She remembers his birthday & asks to go see him
I watched her trace the letters of her name in his headstone
Mia **JULIAN**
She is his namesake

Tears flow down my daughter's face
I give her the stiffest embrace I can muster
Right before we leave she mantles her arms around his marble
structure
Giving it the most solid hug
This is the way she has learned to love

I come from a long line of men whose first love letter was a eulogy
From the era of stop crying before I give you something to cry about
From pick your head up & poke your chest out
Even when you're scared
From boy, you better man up
Black men have always been taught to be tough
Can't never let them see you sweat or cry
We were taught to hide the heavy
Taught to be tough - hard
Inside & out
Taught to never let what's inside out
Or vice-versa
Stand firm
Be Statue
Sometimes that makes us hard, to love
When you're raised in a concrete jungle by a rolling stone
You got no choice but to be rock
The block was our home
No doorbell just hard knocks
It was hard not having a father
But my mother, a Brickhouse
I inherited this cement in my veins
Me & my brother
The more rocks change the more they stay the same
Hard
Us bricks don't fall far from the building

He was every bit of twin tower turned rubble
Every bit of hard head makes soft ass
Hard hat private first class
Couldn't tell him he wasn't part adamantine
Not quite Wolverine, but an X-Man now
Couldn't withstand the storm of bullets to his chest
He was every bit of hard, just not Kevlar
Do you know how solid you have to be to be pillar & pallbearer?
To have to lift him up only to let him down
And still be foundation for family
Still be still
Still be stable, be structure
Can't let them see these cracks
Growing up tight roping the fault lines of an earthquake
We prepare ourselves for the fall
It's bound to happen
So we grow to be hard
Most times, hard to love
When you have brick in your bloodstream can't expect it not to affect
your seeds
My baby girl got gravel in her genes
I don't want her yellow brick road paved in pain
I placed her between a heart & a hard place so she learns to love hard
things, & be just the kinda hard I need her to be,
A gem,
She's beautiful & shining
When you put enough pressure on a rock you make a diamond
She constantly reminding me of how Black women,
regardless of the situation, have always been able to love us,
Hard
I used to avoid letting her see my scars & my tears
I was taught to be tough
To be strong
To protect & provide
Have you ever seen a rock cry?
Then why would I show my daughter that?
To her I am every bit of mountain
She loves me for all that I am
I make sure she understands
Contrary to what she hears
Bricks & stones won't break your bones
They will love you, hug you, squeeze you and raise you to be a
diamond

It's fine if you princess cut into your feelings & learn to love hard things

On Sundays,
We go see her uncle Julian
I Watch her trace the letters of her name in his headstone
Right before we leave
She mantles her arms around his marble structure
Giving it the most solid hug
Between her father, her rock & her uncle, the tombstone
This is how she has learned to love
Hard

HAIKU

SHE JOKED ABOUT MY BALD HEAD
I SAID YOUR MUSTACHE IS CUTE
NOW I'M BLOCKED

Liar Liar: As you read this piece you will notice a similar metaphoric practice as the previous piece. This is a small introduction into the "Artist Brain" I mentioned at the beginning of this book. Sometimes we try so hard to tell a story & don't feel like we get it right, so we attempt to recreate the message in multiple poems. I have three or four different variations of the same story. It stemmed from a moment I noticed my daughter playing with her Legos. Each Lego represented someone in the family. She showed me Nana, Pappy, myself, her Uncle Damon etc. etc., but there was this blue Lego she always kept off to the side. I asked her *"why is the blue one always over there by itself?"* In the most beautifully innocent way. She replied; *"oh, that's Uncle Julian, he never comes over to play with us, we always have to go see him."* I cried like a baby. It was that moment when I realized my baby girl genuinely thought her uncle was the tombstone. I had spent so much time withholding the real truth from her, she began to personify the tombstone.

LIAR LIAR

I've been lying to my daughter

Like most parents do

About Santa Claus

Cuz she'll never have the gift of his presence

If I use the bricks from the chimney

It wouldn't be enough to build a wall to protect my precious little

diamond from the pain on the other side.

So I lied

About the stone-cold truth

A cold case since 2009

A killer probably stoned off crack rocks

Took 4 shots at my brother

Left 4 corners blocked off and my brother lying in the streets,

So I lie to her face

My daughter thinks her uncle is a brick

I am her rock, but there's a million cracks in this foundation

Behind this smile are layers of frozen memories

As I pull his body of ice out of a freezer to identify my mini me

A clear glance at Medusa couldn't make my inner me any harder &

hallow

How low can a man sink before he drowns in his own tears

Rocks don't float they sink

My daughter thinks I can swim

To protect her imagination again, I lie

Like most parents do

About the Easter Bunny

I can't bring my brother back from the dead

I hide the truth like Easter eggs

One day she will find it like they found his killer

That doesn't take the weight off my chest of having to explain

this man's guilt of stealing my baby's innocence by taking her

Uncle's life

She's 4, her perception of family is building blocks stacked on top

of each other with one off to the side

She constantly asking me why he doesn't come over to play

Like any other day, I lie

Like most parents do

About the tooth fairy

Losing a tooth is nothing like losing a sibling

Braces won't close the gap in my family

We bite this truth & swallow the reality

That unlike a missing tooth, he's never coming back

Novocain won't numb the pain of having to explain to my Baby girl

Why she'll never get to see her uncle

But gets to look his killer in the face

How in this case a tooth for a tooth

Still won't replace this cavity in my heart

Dammit, it hurts - 6 years of it

The District Attorney calls & says *"you got your wish,*

We got the guy that killed your brother"

What was I supposed to say?

"Job well done"

Was that supposed to be good news?

That wasn't what I wished for

I wish I had my brother back

I wish my daughter didn't think her uncle was a brick

I wish I didn't have to stick to my deception & lies

But a father's number one job is to be strong, protect & provide

Have you ever seen a rock cry?

Then why would I show my daughter that?

I am her foundation & her uncle was my support beam

Contrary to what you believe

Bricks & stones won't break your bones

They will love you & hug you & squeeze you & raise you to be a diamond

Lying has become a part of parenthood

Or maybe just my excuse to shelter my daughter from the truth

It's time I look her in the face & say

"baby girl I named you Mia Julian after your uncle

He was murdered in cold blood

You'll never get the chance to see his face

Never get to hold his hand

Never get to be engulfed in his embrace

Every Sunday that brick that you hug

It's not really him

It's just the only tangible thing we have left of him for you to love"

HAIKU

HERE ARE TWO PHRASES
THE BAD GUYS DON'T UNDERSTAND
NO. & I CAN'T BREATHE

Questions For The Heavens: This piece is one of those "things that make you go hmmm," pieces. I tend to drift off & write in my head. One rainy, thunderstormy day, I caught myself lost in thought asking myself some of these questions.

Questions For The Heavens

When the entire world is praying, who does God hear first?
Do you think all Gods are friends?
Does your God ask other Gods for favors?
Like can you handle these prayers while I go to lunch?
What's God's favorite food?
Who does God lean on when his heart is heavy?
Do the angels ever check on their strong friends?
Do people still pray in heaven?
Does God kick people out?
Do people get sick?
Are there homeless people?
Does status matter?
Like is my brother hanging out with other murdered angels?
Do you think him, MLK, JFK & Sean Bell take shots together?
No pun intended
Is there still racism?
Do people travel?
Are there beaches?
Is there sunshine on a cloudy day?
Are there cloudy days?
Does it rain?
Do the people still feel pain?
Is there money?
Or has everyone already paid the ultimate price?
Do babies grow?
Do the elderly regain their youth?
No one knows the truth
I'm sure they have questions
If you're not a believer in heaven or hell
That's entirely your choice
I can tell you one thing that will always bring me peace
It will always bring comfort in how I live
I'd rather pray & find out there is no God
Then not pray & find out there is

HAIKU

QUESTIONS ASKED
AFTER GETTING HIGH
CAN CEREAL BE CONSIDERED SOUP

Wish List: I mentioned I have a one-man play titled "I Wish Life Had Training Wheels. I wrote this piece with the intent to use it in the play or as promotion for the play & didn't use it for either. It's been sitting in the archives for a long time. You   are getting its first public appearance.

WISH LIST

The bumps, bruises & BS in life make it so hard to live
It seems like staying alive has become a part of the daily routine
We don't have the dollar & a dream
We get food stamps & nightmares where I'm from
Where the streetlights replace the sun
The only bright spot in our day are the stars at night
I wish I may, I wish I might
I wish life was a book so I can read my next step
I wish my heart could lift weights,
I'd be the strongest man on Earth
Instead of playing the dumbbell, too weak to bench press hurt
I wish life had a map so I'd know which road to follow
I wish tomorrow was promised so I wouldn't miss yesterday
Sometimes life gets in the way
Destiny & faith get replaced with loss & mistakes
It takes a strong man to admit his faults
I wish life had an easy button
I wish frowns didn't exist & pain was just a myth
I wish tears only meant happiness so I can watch my mom cry
everyday
I wish her heart had a hurt vaccine, so my daughter never feels pain
I wish their hearts had a hurt vaccine, so my sons never feel pain
I wish love wasn't so hard to explain
I wish all children knew their fathers
I wish all men took pride in acknowledging their flesh
I wish all tests were graded with a curve & words didn't hurt so much
If a picture is worth a thousand words, then a poem can heal a million
souls
I wish drugs only provided a cure & people became addicted to health
I wish me, myself, I & loneliness had company & misery loved to be
alone
I wish the homeless had windows to look out of
& hate could survive without love
& love could survive without hurt
& happily ever after really worked
I wish life didn't knock you down
I wish luck was in everybody's favor
Father time was my friend
Brother love would proclaim he is my keeper
I wish I was weaker so everyone wouldn't count on me
I wish I was stronger so everyone could count on me
I wish the Angels would look down on me
& the devil got down on his knees & prayed

I wish my brother stayed home that night
I wish I may, I wish I might
I wish some things in life made sense
Like why is gas $7.85 for the cheap stuff
I wish people weren't so scared & kids learned to speak up
I wish life wasn't so tough & all kids played catch with their dads
I wish life wasn't so rough & all kids played catch with their dads
I wish living was just enough, then the dad wouldn't have to play catch
up
I wish enough was really enough & giving in didn't mean giving up
I wish life could hold my hand & help me through it
I wish life had training wheels to help me through it
The bumps, bruises & BS in life make it really hard to live
I wish I really had wishes & could give some of em to you
I wish I may
I wish I might
I wish
I wish
I wish

HAIKU

THOUGHTS AFTER GETTING HIGH
DO I WORK FROM HOME
OR DO I LIVE AT WORK

Last Night's Prayer: I often try to avoid the news as it rarely displays the positive of our society. Yet social media has claimed the title for negative publications. I browse & see the horrible injustices happening in Palestine & various continents & countries outside of the United States & my heart aches for the people. It aches for the babies & families. I'm not wealthy enough to assist in any real change. Sometimes I feel like all I am left with is prayer & protest. Since people with my skin aren't always successful or safe during protest, my last option is to pray.

Last Night's Prayer

We live in a world where we can't even pray in peace
Our peace has become their prey
When being openly gay causes hate to spray bullets through a
nightclub
They instantly disclose the shooter's religion as if Christians don't kill
If I said the Lord's prayer in Arabic does that make me a terrorist

Last night I prayed in silence
Heard buildings crumble in Gaza
Screams in France - Children crying in LA
Heard sirens in Kuwait - Gunshots in Hartford
21 trumpets playing Taps as we salute the Frenchman
Carrying a dead Palestinian child wrapped in an American Flag
Someone assigned a color to life
Someone attached hate to a Religion
Someone thinks their opinion means more than our prayers

Last night I prayed for Palestine
Doesn't matter which God I prayed to
I prayed for the innocent lives eradicated over a hatred that no one can
explain
MLK proclaimed hate cannot drive out hate, only love can do that
Well, who put the hate there in the first place?
How much love does it take to get to the center of a terrorist?

Last night I prayed for world peace
Or at least for the piece of the world I live in to be safe
What do you do when you see fear in the face of your pastor?
When you have nothing left in life to believe in
Grieving becomes the chapter of your life that never ends
Like death, violence & time
People blown to pieces before they can pick them up from the last
bomb dropped
A bomb cannot stop a bomb
Only... well, I don't have an answer for that

Last night I prayed for answers
It doesn't matter who I prayed to
Prayer is a universal language
Like pain
It's spoken in tears
Blood stains are a different dialect
Black bags are Ebonics

Don't you find it ironic that dead bodies are covered in white sheets &
transfer to black bags
I guess that's what it takes for blacks & whites to work together
How dare we assign a color to life?
We call our immigrants illegal aliens
What will we name the real aliens when they come?
Will their lives matter?
Will they be considered the new terrorist so we can finally leave
Muslims alone
Our former president said...
Did you really think I would quote politics in my poem?

Last night I prayed for Peace
I prayed for all those people we forget to mention today that we
marched for last week
You can't be an activist just following trends
It makes you an actor
You pretend to be someone that cares
Prayer is a verb, an action word
Doesn't matter who you pray to, the least you can do is pray
For a better day
For a better people
For a better tomorrow
If you're not a praying person
Then use one of them wishes from the genie in the bottle
Cuz prayer, wishes & hope is all we have
We is the key word
When we band together, we work
Towards greatness & no matter the holiday or celebration
This is an open call for prayer
Consider it an invitation

To help the world be a better place

HAIKU

STILL JUDGED BY HER HEADWRAP
OUR 9/11
IS HER 24/7

WHERE IM FROM II: I've always embraced where I'm From. I proudly represent being from a small city in one of the smallest states. I've performed poetry in many states where people sincerely did not believe there were Black people in Connecticut. The pieces dedicated to my hometown of 'Hard Hittin' New Britain Connecticut serve as an educator to those who assume such things.

WHERE IM FROM II

I wrote a poem called where I'm from
You ask why would I write the same poem again?
Because where I'm from the more things change the more they don't
This ain't the same poem, this is yesterday
Where I'm from kids either work the block or work on their jump shot
Or they stay in the house because they fear getting jumped or shot
When parents complain their kids are addicted to video games
I tell them, it's better than drugs
Where I'm from there's a constant cycle of defeat
Student cusses out teacher
Teacher tells parent
Parent blames teacher
Student never learns
Where's the lesson in that?
Where I'm from you get more compliments on your sneakers then your vocabulary
More concerned with getting J's instead of A's
They get more love when they come home from prison instead of college
Only time they're woke is at a wake
Then again, my people don't respect life or death
They fight at funerals & pour out liquor for the pregnant girls that can't party with them instead of the dead homies
Where I'm from the dead homie's mom couldn't afford a home going ceremony
He just went home
No funeral or tombstone
Just an RIP Facebook post
Where I'm from gone too soon tattoos are the first badge of honor
PS, we still don't know who killed him
Which is ironic because where I'm from snitches don't always get stitches, they get paroled
No one wants to face the truth
When little girl tells on mommy's boyfriend mom asks her for proof
She can't tell her father cuz that's mommy's boyfriend
Now she's stuck between pills & a noose
I know that may be triggering to say in a poem, but the truth hurts
I'd rather the truth hurt you than the people
Where I'm from the father didn't raise his son,
the son didn't raise his son
We called them the senior in the sequel
If the baby has a baby, we pray he won't be the trilogy

What's killing me is this ain't the same poem
This is history repeating itself
This ain't the same poem, it's a eulogy for your past, a love letter to
your future
Where I'm from everyone is used to the same ole same
No one dares to break the cycle
I dare you to be the difference, I dare you to be different
I know the pain is right in front of you, but Glory is in the distance
There will always be bumps in the road, but you Gotta be consistent
Where I'm from isn't as bad as people always make it seem was already
written
This ain't the same poem, it's a prescription for success
Call it dedication medication
Use it to remind you that where you're from shouldn't be your only &
final destination
You gotta dream big, way outside of your city & state
There's an entire world out there waiting for you to take it
Where you're from shouldn't be your excuse
It should be the reason why you make it

HAIKU

DEADBEAT DAD
RASIED A DEABEAT SON
WE CALL THEM SENIOR & THE SEQUEL

Male Ego: Poet extraordinaire, Kayo, introduced me to poetic theater & allowed me to be a part of the stage play "The Male Ego." I worked with brilliant writers & musicians to create a masterful story of male fragility & the dynamics of ego. We toured & had an amazing time sharing our stories with the world. This piece was used as an opener to the showcase.

MALE EGO

Put yourself in my shoes & imagine what it's like to be viewed like every other dude

Take a walk in my Nike's & imagine what it's like to have the psyche of a male in adversity

Understood universally as a dog, liar, cheater, a graduate of player university

Summa Cum Loser, Magna Cum Liar with no desire to be a one-woman man

Commitment is something that doesn't come easy

Learning what the word commit meant was something daddy could never teach me

Take a walk in our shoes, would you even be able to stand?

Or are you truly confused about what makes a male a man?

Call it a miscommunication, confusion or hate

The topic of male vs. man is up for debate

On behalf of us men I'll speak

For you males, I'll translate

Being a man does not, I repeat, does not MANifest on its own

There's no MANual or MANuscript

You've used the MALE-practice of MANaging your MANners inappropriately

Thinking its MANdatory to run your MANdible using different MANeuvers to control the minds of MANkind

Assuming your MANhood is defined by your ability to MANipulate women

Believing because you paid for a MANicure

that you are now the MAN

You male-function to realize that the length of your penis can never be compared to the strength of your genius

Pull up your pants & put down your wallet cuz it credits those that cash in on knowledge

Mama didn't raise no fool,

Daddy was the dummy that never raised me & it made me the MAN I am today

Put yourself in my shoes & take a walk this way

Where most men are afraid to be fathers cuz they didn't have one of their own

Afraid to be husbands cuz papa was a rolling stone

Scared to be men cuz the little boy inside has never grown

Throughout life they been shown the wrong way to live, but the right way to lie

How to take & not give & real men don't cry

Put yourself in our shoes & you might understand why

We're forced to be tough & tell lies

Cockiness covers up the lack of confidence we hide

Pride sometimes gets the best of us, ego consumes the rest of us

Being a MAN is just a test for us that all men must take

Eventually we'll all pass

Experience will be the excuse we can name our mistakes

Fool me once shame on you, fool me twice, shame on me, fool me 3times, that's just a damn shame

Together we represent a MAN'S name & every aspect of it

The insecurity, immaturity, infidelity, promiscuity,

The loving, passionate, caring, controlling yet consoling parts of a man are all what make me, we, us, MEN

We can't pretend that they're something they're not

The content of their character can't be something they've got from the streets

Taught to be too tough to shed tears, admit you were wrong, apologize & mean it

Let your little brother win

It's not a sin to be smart or to start showing some love

Above all else remember your self-respect

Don't neglect that if you want it you, have to give it

Because you live there, doesn't mean you live it

Being male doesn't make you a MAN

Until you understand you have to acknowledge your abilities &

accept your flaws

The laws of nature have confirmed

That stubbornness is a must & sensitivity is illegal

This is a story of a MAN emerging from his ego

HAIKU

ELECTRIC SLIDE WOBBLE SWAG SURF
THE ONLY TIME
BLACKS WORK TOGETHER

Learning Is From Experience: I thought there would be no better way to end these passages than by using one of the poems that started it all. The bitter break up blues has catapulted many careers & it was absolutely the catalyst to my poetry/spoken word journey. If you read it carefully you notice it is an ode & a thank you to my past.

L.I.F.E.

Although
Loneliness is still around
I continue to live life with half of a smile
With faith that
Love is still awaiting
For me to cross its path
Life is so amazing
When you have someone to share it with
Learned that from a
Lady I shooed away
Luckily I stayed around
Long enough to learn that a real woman needs a real man
Now I understand I was only half the man she needed
I was half the man, with half a smile giving half ass effort which
left me
Living in sadness & loneliness is still around
Lately I've slept alone
Because I was worried about hanging with the fellas & never
Acknowledged she is lonely
Finally, when I decided to make time she felt like she was
Laying in a stranger's arms
Out of nowhere
Love's invisible spirit appeared
Teaching me
Love isn't scattered affection
After that reality set in,
I attempted to make it better, display emotions,
Provide romance, do all the little things
That was after the fact

After sure is late when love is slipping away

I should have

Listened instead of argued

Loved instead of abandoned

I avoided signs in love

And Suddenly I'm lost

I spent months in pain

Reminiscing on the beauty of being in love

The days when I had someone special to share life with

Even with many regrets

I continue to live on with half of a smile & faith that

Love is still awaiting

For me to cross its path

I've learned from my mistakes

A second in love

Is all it takes for anyone to realize how beautiful life can be

I learned that from a

Lady I shoved away

She has taught me even with the bitterness of falling out

Love is so amazing

I can't wait to love again

HAIKU

BEAUTIFUL WOMAN
ONCE INTRODUCED ME TO LOVE
THEN SHE BROKE MY HEART

Thank you

Thank you all for investing your time into my world.

Please tap into my podcast **All Black Men Need Therapy**, on all streaming platforms as well as YouTube. Much of my journey in writing has derived from my growth in therapy. I've learned that I don't know what I don't know, but what I do know, is we carry a weight that can be lessened if we just talk about it.

About the author

Michael "Chief" Peterson marries social consciousness with mellow poetic verses. Born & raised in New Britain, CT, he declares himself a man dedicated to his family & focused on helping our youth. Chief not only speaks about social inequities & individual struggle, but he acts to change the cycle. Chief is the playwright of & actor in his one-man show, *I Wish Life Had Training Wheels*. He was appointed as the first ever Poet Laureate of his hometown, New Britain, Connecticut in which he was recently appointed to a second term. He appeared on Seasons 4,5, & 6 of the TvOne hit series, *Lexus' Verses and Flow*. He is a 3x Connecticut Spoken Word Grand Slam Champion as well as a coach for the CT youth & adult poetry Slam teams.

Chief was featured at the Kallio Block Party in Helsinki, Finland. He also performed at the 2012 London Olympics. Chief has also performed with Brian Mcknight, Ginuwine & Musiq Soul Child during The Love Heart & Soul tour.

A graduate of the University of Rhode Island with a Bachelor of Arts in Elementary Education & a Bachelor's degree in Child Psychology, as well as a Master's degree in Educational Leadership from Central Connecticut State University, Chief is no stranger to the injustice he speaks out about. He is currently a Dean of Students at his alma mater, New Britain High School, & is also a part-time Child Development Specialist.

From the high school where he works to the stages where he performs, this poet on the rise turns his art into action while inspiring people to do the same. This is a performer who literally practices what he preaches. From the high school where he works to the stages where he performs, this poet on the rise is about turning his art into action & inspiring people to do the same.

To my children,

I never wanted to create a book until I had 'something to say.' With all the stages I've been on & all the people I've inspired, I still felt like I didn't have a message worthy enough to put in a book. I had a world of people around me encouraging me to get my poems out there. I struggled with them not being "enough." In many cases, I was my own hardest critic. I've learned self-doubt can destroy dreams. I still intend to put out a book that delivers the specific message I intend it to. Until that time comes, this collection is a reminder to always believe in yourself, to stand firm in your vulnerability & discomfort & that sometimes, done, is better than perfect. Sometimes, your message is just what the world needs, right when they need it. Always stand firm in your beliefs in who you are. Dare to be brave enough to step out of your comfort zone. YOU, are the message the world needs. Anything else you bring shall be considered a blessing to anyone who experiences it.

POETS

MAKING

IMMORTAL

#MAKING

310 BROWN
.com
STREET

PUBLISHING

310brownstreet.com

@310brownstreet

www.ingramcontent.com/pod-product-compliance
Lightning Source LLC
Chambersburg PA
CBHW020210090426
42734CB00008B/1011